This book belongs to:

....

Published by C&T Publishing, Inc.
P.O. Box 1456, Lafayette, CA 94549

www.ctpub.com

ISBN 978-1-60705-759-8

Designed in the U.S.A. Printed in China.

10 9 8 7 6 5 4 3 2 1

Cover quilt by Maxine Rosenthal

This page quilt by Rayna Gillman

Previous page quilt by Caryl Bryer Fallert-Gentry

ARTISTS

Alex Anderson	Judy Mathieson
Allie Aller	Judy Sisneros
Anelie Belden	Kathe Dougherty
Anita Grossman Solomon	Katie Pasquini Masopust
Anna Faustino	Kim Schaefer
Barbara H. Cline	Linda Jenkins
Becky Goldsmith	Louisa L. Smith
Bobbi Finley	Maxine Rosenthal
Caryl Bryer Fallert-Gentry	Norah McMeeking
Claudia Clark Myers	Pam Goecke Dinndorf
Deborah Kemball	Paula Nadelstern
Elizabeth Barton	Rayna Gillman
Geta Grama	Ricky Tims
Gloria Loughman	Ruth B. McDowell
Grace Errea	Sally Collins
Jan Krentz	Sue Beevers
Jan Sheets	Susan Brubaker Knapp
Jean Wells	Susan Carlson
Joan Colvin	Thom Atkins
Joen Wolfrom	Valerie S. Goodwin
John Flynn	Wendy Mathson

Detail of *Happy Houses* by Bobbi Finley quilted by Holly Casey, from *Fresh Perspectives* by Bobbi Finley and Carol Jones, 70½" × 70½"

1

2

3

4

5

6

7

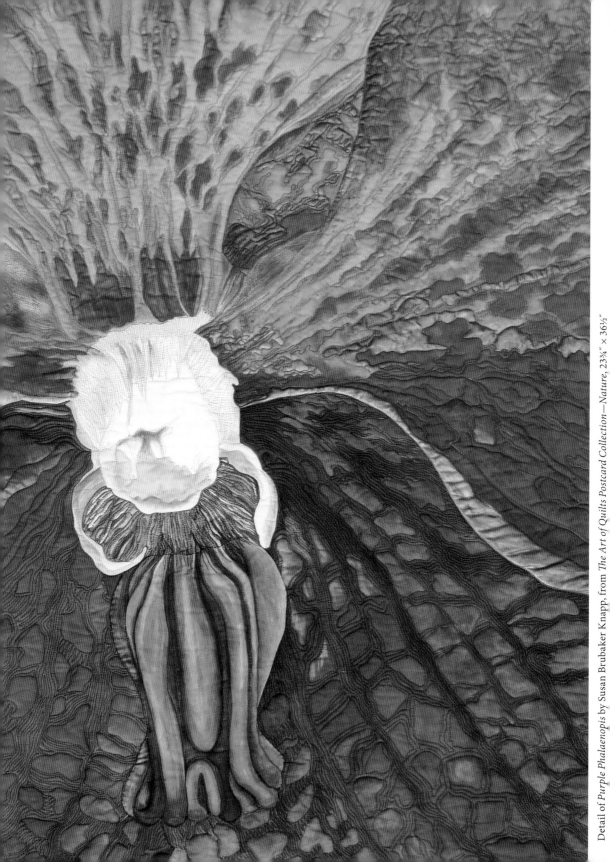

8

9

10

11

12

13

14

15

16

17

18

19

20

21

Detail of *All in a Dream* by Kathe Dougherty quilted by Lori Kukuk, from *Tile Quilt Revival* by Bobbi Finley and Carol Jones, 74" × 74"

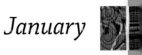

22

23

24

25

26

27

28

Detail of *Sticks and Stones* by Alex Anderson quilted by Paula Reid, from *Intuitive Color and Design* by Jean Wells, 43½" × 47"

29

30

31

Detail of *Robins* by Joan Colvin, from *Nature's Studio*, 62" × 29"

1

2

3

4

5

6

7

Detail of Queen Allie's Lace *by Allie Aller, from Allie Aller's Crazy Quilting, 20" × 20"*

February

8

9

10

11

12

13

14

15

16

17

18

19

20

21

22

23

24

25

26

27

28

Ruth B. McDowell

Detail of *Fort Morrison Jerseys* by Ruth B. McDowell, from *A Fabric Journey*, photography by David Caras, 65½″ × 46″

Detail of *Flower Power Dresden Sampler* by Anelie Belden, from *Thoroughly Modern Dresden*, 48½″ × 54½″

1

2

3

4

5

6

7

8

9

10

11

12

13

14

Detail of *Dancing Feathers* by Geta Grama, from *Shadow Trapunto Quilts*, photography by Dan Comaniciu, 37½″ × 38½″

15

16

17

18

19

20

21

22

23

24

25

26

27

28

29

30

31

Detail of *Small Wonder* by Jean Wells, from *Journey to Inspired Art Quilting*, 24" × 24"

1

2

3

4

5

6

7

8

9

10

11

12

13

14

Detail of *Block 8: Dots* by Paula Nadelstern, from *Kaleidoscope Quilts—The Workbook*, 20" × 20"

15

16

17

18

19

20

21

22

23

24

25

26

27

28

Detail of *Red* by Maxine Rosenthal, from *One-Block Wonders*, 64" × 78"

29

30

May

1

2

3

4

5

6

7

8

9

10

11

12

13

14

Detail of *Paint* by Katie Pasquini Masopust, from *Design Explorations for the Creative Quilter*, photography by Wendy McGerin, 60" × 45"

15

16

17

18

19

20

21

22

- -

23

- -

24

- -

25

- -

26

- -

27

- -

28

- -

29

30

31

Detail of *Spiral Lone Star* by Jan Krentz, from *Lone Star Quilts & Beyond*, photography by Carina Woolrich, 46" × 46"

1

2

3

4

5

6

7

8

9

10

11

12

13

14

15

16

17

18

19

20

21

22

23

24

25

26

27

28

Detail of *Fructos* by Susan Carlson, from *Serendipity Quilts*, collection of Sylvia Dyer, photography by Dennis Griggs of Tannery Hill Studios, 36″ × 39½″

29

30

Detail of *Sedona* by Sally Collins, from *Drafting for the Creative Quilter*, 45½" × 45½"

1

2

3

4

5

6

7

Detail of *Bow Ties* by Alex Anderson quilted by Diane Schweickert, from *Scrap Quilting with Alex Anderson*, 56½" × 56½"

8

9

10

11

12

13

14

15

16

17

18

19

20

21

Detail of *Tenuous Membrane* by Thom Atkins, from *Beading Artistry for Quilts*, 29" × 44"

22

23

24

25

26

27

28

29

30

31

Detail of *Under the Sea* by Barbara H. Cline, from *Diamond Chain Quilts*, 49" × 48"

August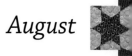

1

2

3

4

5

6

7

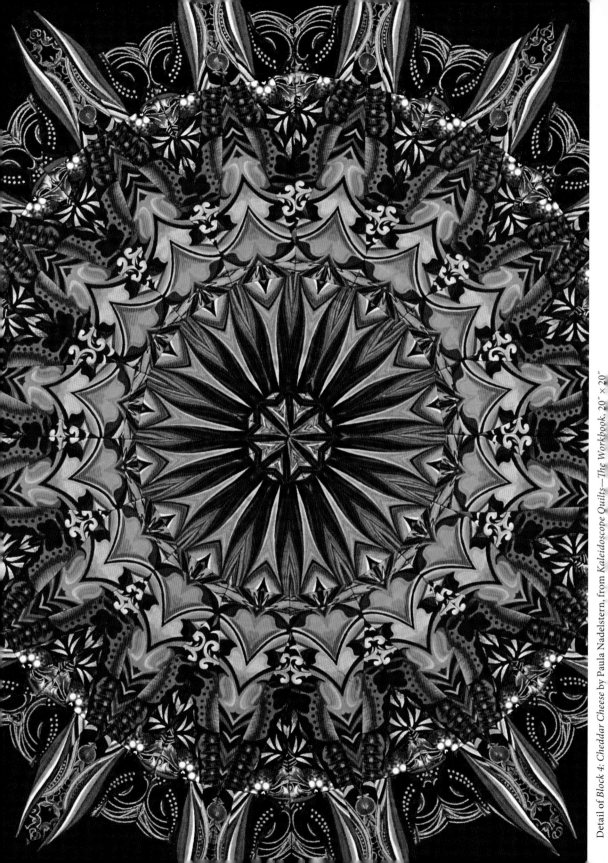

Detail of *Block 4: Cheddar Cheese* by Paula Nadelstern, from *Kaleidoscope Quilts—The Workbook*. 20" × 20"

8

9

10

11

12

13

14

Detail of *Wisteria Arbor* by Sue Beevers, from *Dancing Dragonfly Quilts*, 81" × 108"

15

16

17

18

19

20

21

Detail of *Turkish Delight* by Judy Sisneros, from *Circle Pizzazz*, 47" × 56½"

22

23

24

25

26

27

28

Detail of *Blowin' in the Wind* by Becky Goldsmith, from *The Best-Ever Appliqué Sampler from Piece O' Cake Designs* by Becky Goldsmith and Linda Jenkins, 48" × 48"

29

30

31

1

2

3

4

5

6

7

Detail of *Any Port in a Storm* by Wendy Mathson quilted by Faith Horsky, from *A New Light on Storm at Sea Quilts*, 72″ × 90″

8

9

10

11

12

13

14

Detail of *Life After the Storm* by Grace Errea, from *Impressionist Appliqué* by Grace Errea and Meridith Osterfeld, photography by Dan Snipes, 49" × 51"

15

16

17

18

19

20

21

Detail of *Tenacious* by Sally Collins, from *Drafting for the Creative Quilter*, 23" × 23"

22

23

24

25

26

27

28

Detail of *Ode to Michael* by Louisa L. Smith, from *A New Twist on Strips 'n Curves, 40" x 40"*

29

30

1

2

3

4

5

6

7

Detail of *Blue Moon* by Claudia Clark Myers quilted by Marilyn Badger, from *A Passion for Piecing*, 81" × 81"

October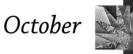

8

9

10

11

12

13

14

Detail of *Early Frost* by Rayna Gillman, from *Create Your Own Hand-Printed Cloth*, 35" × 32"

15

16

17

18

19

20

21

Detail of *Sticks and Stones* by Jean Wells, from *Journey to Inspired Art Quilting*, 16½" × 28½"

22

23

24

25

26

27

28

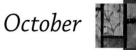
29

30

31

Detail of *Palampore Tree of Life* by Deborah Kemball, from *Beautiful Botanicals*. 50½″ × 50½″

November

1

2

3

4

5

6

7

November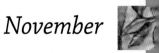

8

9

10

11

12

13

14

Detail of *ArchiTEXTural cARTography* by Valerie S. Goodwin, from *Art Quilt Maps*, 36″ × 50″

15

16

17

18

19

20

21

Detail of *LeMoyne Star Appliqué Medallion* by Alex Anderson quilted by Paula Reid, from *Neutral Essentials with Alex Anderson,* 45½" × 45½"

22

23

24

25

26

27

28

29

30

1

2

3

4

5

6

7

8

9

10

11

12

13

14

Detail of *Christmas in the Park* by Linda Jenkins quilted by Mary Covey, from *Quilt a New Christmas with Piece O' Cake Designs* by Becky Goldsmith and Linda Jenkins, 45" × 61"

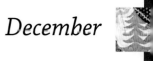

15

16

17

18

19

20

21

December

22

23

24

25

26

27

28

29
- -

30
- -

31
- -

Anniversary Gifts
BY YEAR

YEAR	TRADITIONAL	MODERN	ALTERNATE	FLOWERS	GEM STONES
1	Paper	Plastic	Clocks	Pansy	Gold Jewelry ALT: Peridot
2	Cotton	Cotton and Calico	China	Cosmos	Garnet
3	Leather	Leather	Crystal and Glass	Fuchsia	Pearls ALT: Jade
4	Fruit and Flowers	Linen, Silk, Nylon	Appliances	Geranium	Blue Topaz ALT: Blue Zircon
5	Wood	Wood	Silverware	Daisy	Sapphire ALT: Pink Tourmaline
6	Candy	Iron	Wood	Calla Lily	Amethyst ALT: Turquoise
7	Copper and Wool	Brass	Desk Sets	Jack-in-the-Pulpit	Onyx ALT: Yellow Sapphire
8	Bronze	Pottery	Linen	Clematis	Tourmaline ALT: Tanzanite
9	Pottery	Willow	Leather	Poppy	Lapis Lazuli ALT: Amethyst
10	Tin	Aluminum	Diamond	Daffodil	Diamond ALT: Blue Sapphire

YEAR	TRADITIONAL	MODERN	ALTERNATE	FLOWERS	GEM STONES
11	Steel	Steel	Jewelry	Morning Glory	Turquoise ALT: Citrine
12	Silk	Linen	Pearl	Peony	Jade ALT: Opal
13	Lace	Lace	Textiles, Faux Fur	Hollyhock	Citrine ALT: Moonstone, Hawk's Eye
14	Ivory	Ivory	Gold	Dahlia	Opal ALT: Agate, Bloodstone
15	Crystal	Glass	Watches	Rose	Ruby ALT: Alexandrite, Rhodolite Garnet
16		Silver Holloware			Peridot ALT: Red Spinel
17		Furniture			Watch ALT: Carnelian
18		Porcelain			Cat's Eye or Chrysoberyl
19		Bronze			Aquamarine ALT: Almandine Garnet
20	China	China	Platinum	Day Lily	Emerald ALT: Yellow or Golden Diamond
21		Brass and Nickel			Iolite
22		Copper			Spinel
23		Silver Plate			Imperial Topaz
24		Musical Instruments			Tanzanite
25	Silver	Silver	Silver	Iris	Silver Jubilee

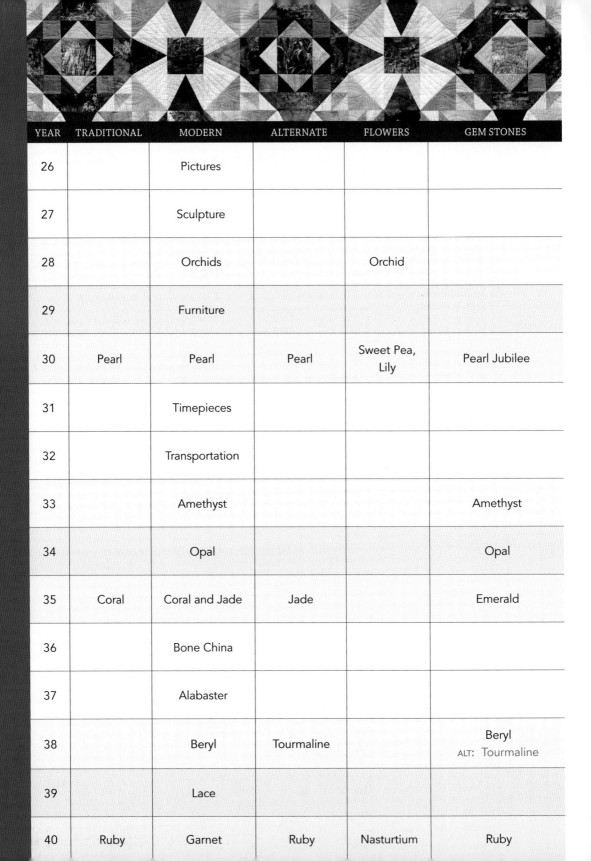

YEAR	TRADITIONAL	MODERN	ALTERNATE	FLOWERS	GEM STONES
26		Pictures			
27		Sculpture			
28		Orchids		Orchid	
29		Furniture			
30	Pearl	Pearl	Pearl	Sweet Pea, Lily	Pearl Jubilee
31		Timepieces			
32		Transportation			
33		Amethyst			Amethyst
34		Opal			Opal
35	Coral	Coral and Jade	Jade		Emerald
36		Bone China			
37		Alabaster			
38		Beryl	Tourmaline		Beryl ALT: Tourmaline
39		Lace			
40	Ruby	Garnet	Ruby	Nasturtium	Ruby

YEAR	TRADITIONAL	MODERN	ALTERNATE	FLOWERS	GEM STONES
41		Land			
42		Real Estate			
43		Travel			
44		Gourmet			
45	Sapphire	Sapphire	Sapphire		Cat's Eye
46		Poetry			
47		Books			
48		Optical			
49		Luxury Goods			
50	Gold	Gold	Gold	Violet	Golden Jubilee ALT: Imperial or Golden Topaz
55	Emerald	Turquoise	Emerald		Alexandrite
60	Diamond	Gold	Diamond		Diamond Jubilee ALT: Star Ruby
65	Diamond	Gold	Diamond		Blue Spinel
70	Diamond	Gold	Diamond		Sapphire Jubilee ALT: Smoky Quartz
75	Diamond	Gold	Diamond		Diamond Jubilee
80		Diamond			Ruby Jubilee

Birthstones

- JANUARY
  Garnet

- FEBRUARY
  Amethyst

- MARCH
  Aquamarine
  Bloodstone

- APRIL
  Diamond

- MAY
  Emerald

- JUNE
  Pearl
  Alexandrite
  Moonstone

- JULY
  Ruby

- AUGUST
  Peridot

- SEPTEMBER
  Sapphire

- OCTOBER
  Tourmaline
  Opal

- NOVEMBER
  Topaz
  Citrine

- DECEMBER
  Tanzanite
  Zircon
  Turquoise

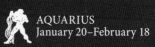
AQUARIUS
January 20–February 18

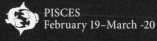
PISCES
February 19–March -20

ARIES
March 21–April 19

TAURUS
April 20–May 20

GEMINI
May 21–June 20

CANCER
June 21–July 22

LEO
July 23–August 22

VIRGO
August 23–September 22

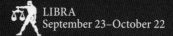
LIBRA
September 23–October 22

SCORPIO
October 23–November 21

SAGITTARIUS
November 22–December 21

CAPRICORN
December 22–January 19

My Family Tree

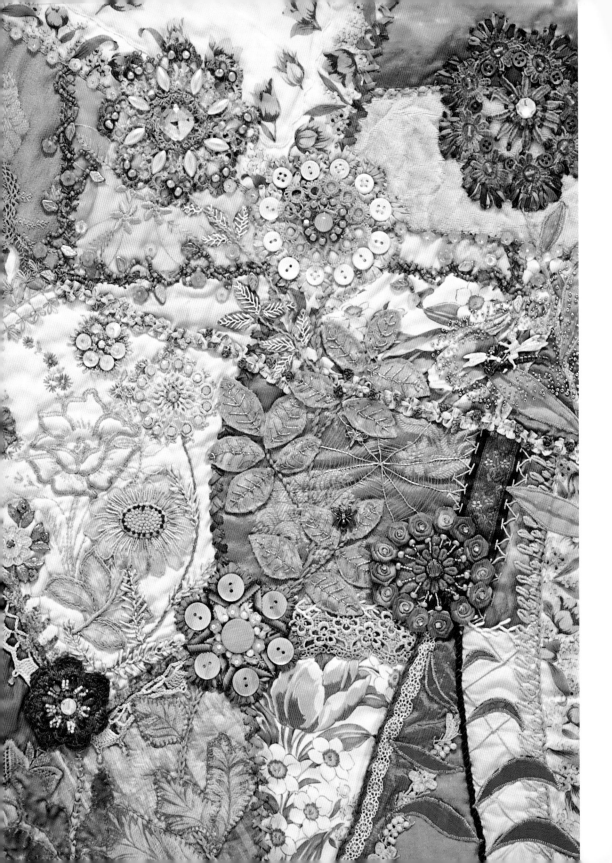

Flowers
by month

JANUARY
Carnations and snowdrops

FEBRUARY
Violet and the primrose

MARCH
Daffodils and jonquils

APRIL
Daisies and sweet peas

MAY
Lily of the valley and hawthorn

JUNE
Roses and honeysuckles

JULY
Larkspur and water lilies

AUGUST
Gladiolus and poppy

SEPTEMBER
Aster and morning glory

OCTOBER
Marigolds and cosmos

NOVEMBER
Chrysanthemums

DECEMBER
Narcissus and holly

notes

notes

notes